MONSTER MAZE MADNESS

By Jacques Chazaud

tempo books

GROSSET & DUNLAP
A FILMWAYS COMPANY
Publishers • New York

To Lois,
   Jeanne,
   Nicole,
   Henri
   and Marc

Compiled from MONSTER MAZES and
MORE MONSTER MAZES

What has over 3000 teeth, 234 fangs, 431 legs, 25 wings, 34 tentacles and bad breath?

Why it's MONSTER MAZE MADNESS, of course!

To solve these puzzles, just take a pencil and start where the arrow points the way in. Then, find the one path that will take you to the exit without crossing any of the solid lines.

For extra fun, see if you can better the challenge time given for each maze. Don't despair if the first one you try seems hard. You may slither through another one in half the rated time.

If you wish to keep your monster mazes clean, for your friends to solve or for you to color, simply lay a sheet of tracing paper over the mazes before you begin.

So let's go. The monsters are waiting!

Solutions appear in the back of the book.

Maze 1
HOME, SWEET HOME
Challenge Time / 2:00

Maze 2

ARIES

Challenge Time / 2:10

Maze 3

VIPER'S NEST

Challenge Time / 50 Seconds

Maze 4

SSSSSSSSS

Challenge Time / 1:30

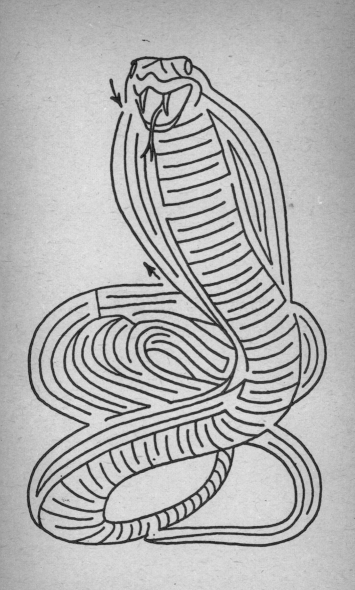

Maze 5

WARLOCK'S MOON
Challenge Time / 55 Seconds

Maze 6

TAURUS

Challenge Time / 1:25

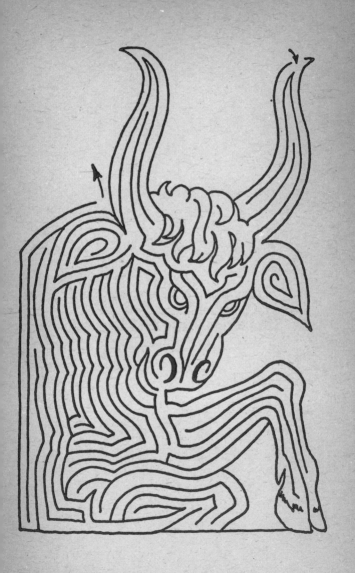

Maze 7
WITCH DOCTOR
Challenge Time / 55 Seconds

Maze 8
THE PERILS OF PAPUA
Challenge Time / 1:50

Maze 9
THE MINOTAUR'S MAZE
Challenge Time / 1:10

Maze 10
GEMINI
Challenge Time / 3:30

Maze 11
TIRED TRICERATOPS
Challenge Time / 1:15

Maze 12

SQUEEZE PLAY

Challenge Time / 1:35

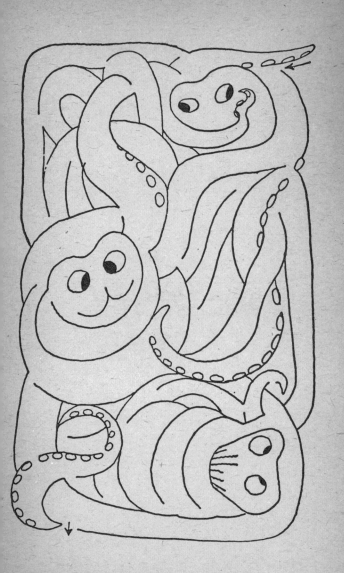

Maze 13
TOAD
Challenge Time / 1:25

Maze 14
CANCER
Challenge Time / 1:45

Maze 15

WITCH'S BREW

Challenge Time / 1:45

Maze 16
GODZILLA
Challenge Time / 1:44

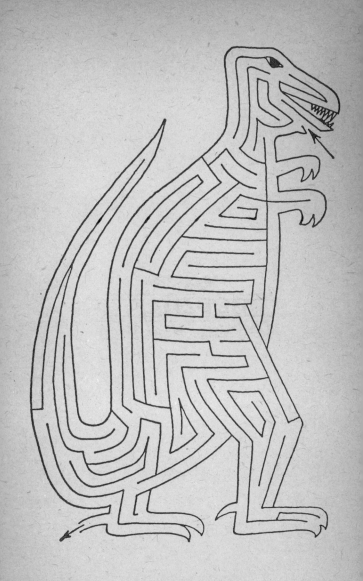

Maze **17**

WHAT SMELLS?

Challenge Time / 1:40

Maze 18

RAT TRAP

Challenge Time / 1:45

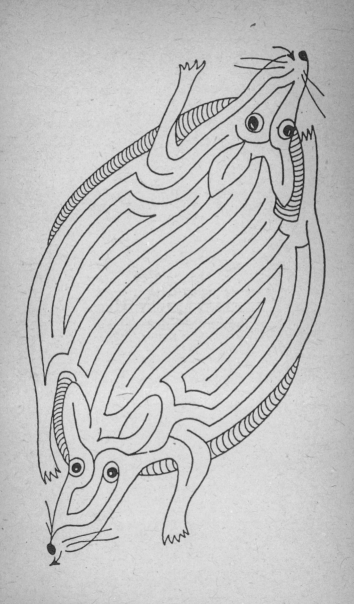

Maze 19
LEO
Challenge Time / 2:30

Maze 20
WANNA FIGHT?
Challenge Time / 2:05

Maze 21

GET OUT OF HERE!

Challenge Time / 1:50

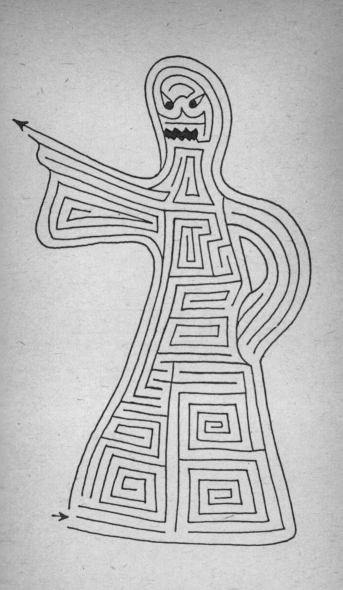

Maze 22
DEVILTRY
Challenge Time / 4:41

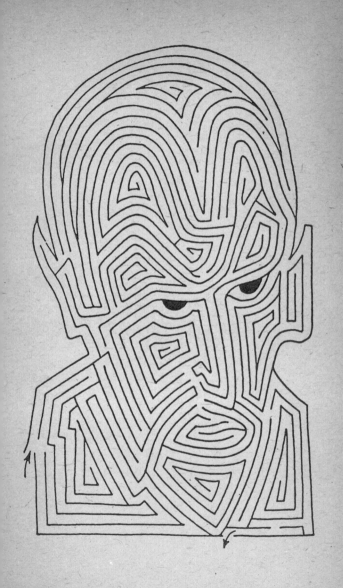

Maze 23
WHEEEEE!!
Challenge Time / 2:05

Maze 24
VIRGO
Challenge Time / 4:40

Maze 25

GORGONZOLA

Challenge Time / 1:50

Maze 26
BIG BURP
Challenge Time / 2:25

Maze 27

IN ONE EAR &
OUT THE OTHER

Challenge Time / 1:55

Maze 28
LIBRA
Challenge Time / 2:30

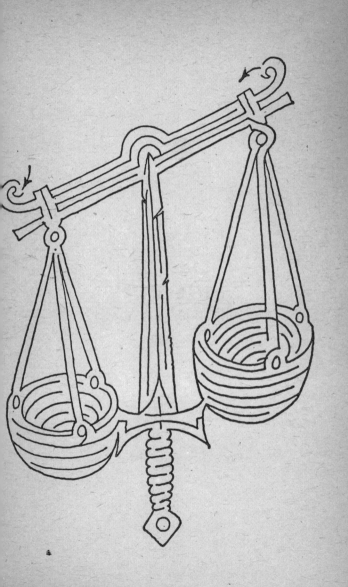

Maze 29
EVIL VIAL
Challenge Time / 2:30

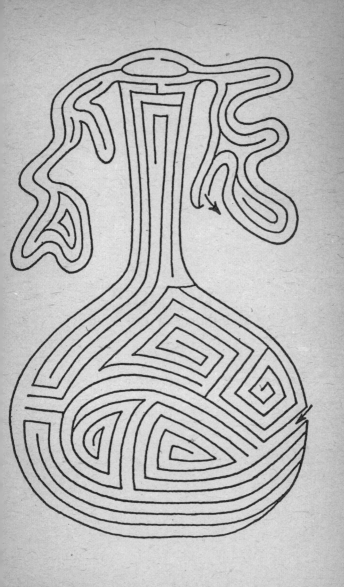

Maze 30

GRENDEL

Challenge Time / 1:55

Maze 31
STINK IN SAMOA
Challenge Time / 2:35

Maze 32

SCORPIO

Challenge Time / 3:00

Maze 33

WEREWOLF

Challenge Time / 2:41

Maze 34

OLD SKI NOSE

Challenge Time / 1:55

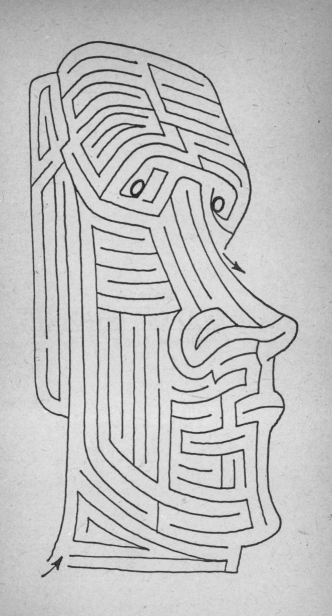

Maze 35
LOVE FROM FRANKIE
Challenge Time / 3:00

Maze 36

SAGITTARIUS

Challenge Time / 2:25

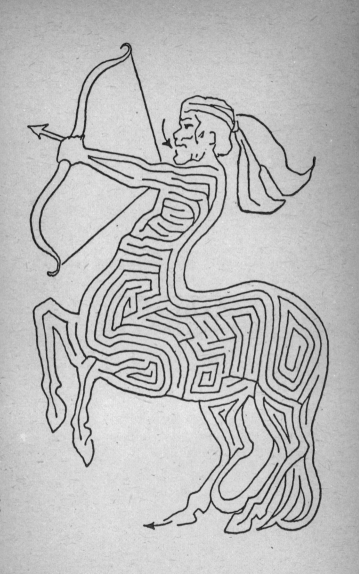

Maze 37
CAPTAIN KIDD
Challenge Time / 3:05

Maze 38
SPINACH AGAIN?
Challenge Time / 2:00

Maze 39

WHAT DO YOU MEAN, "WE'RE MARRIED"?

Challenge Time / 2:20

Maze 40

LOCH NESS

Challenge Time / 2:00

Maze 41

CLUE: BOO!

Challenge Time / 3:30

Maze 42
CAPRICORN
Challenge Time / 1:10

Maze 43

GOOD NIGHT!

Challenge Time / 2:05

Maze 44

CRYSTAL BALL

Challenge Time / 3:30

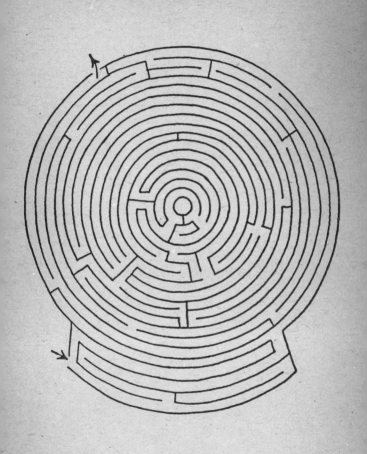

Maze 45

AQUARIUS

Challenge Time / 2:55

Maze 46

BLINK

Challenge Time / 2:30

Maze 47

MA GRIFFE

Challenge Time / 2:20

Maze 48
WHIZZARD
Challenge Time / 5:30

Maze 49

PISCES

Challenge Time / 2:25

Maze 50

DINNER TIME

Challenge Time / 1:30

1. HOME, SWEET HOME

2. ARIES

3. VIPER'S NEST

4. SSSSSSSSS

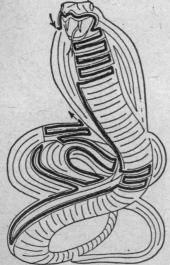

5. WARLOCK'S MOON

6. TAURUS

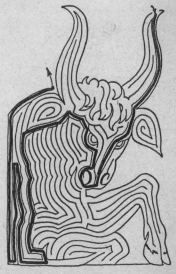

7. WITCH DOCTOR

8. THE PERILS OF PAPUA

9. THE MINOTAUR'S MAZE

10. GEMINI

11. TIRED TRICERATOPS

12. SQUEEZE PLAY

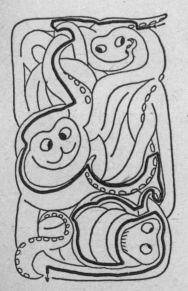

13. TOAD

14. CANCER

15. WITCH'S BREW

16. GODZILLA

17. WHAT SMELLS?

18. RAT TRAP

19. LEO

20. WANNA FIGHT?

21. GET OUT OF HERE!

22. DEVILTRY

23. WHEEEEEE!!

24. VIRGO

25. GORGONZOLA

26. BIG BURP

**27. IN ONE EAR &
OUT THE OTHER**

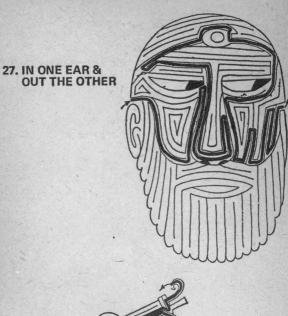

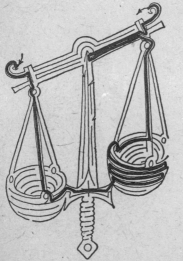

28. LIBRA

29. EVIL VIAL

30. GRENDEL

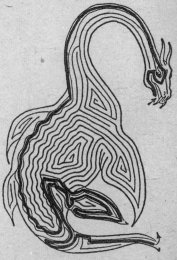

31. STINK IN SAMOA

32. SCORPIO

33. WEREWOLF

34. OLD SKI NOSE

35. LOVE FROM FRANKIE

36. SAGITTARIUS

37. CAPTAIN KIDD

38. SPINACH AGAIN?

39. WHAT DO YOU MEAN, "WE'RE MARRIED"?

40. LOCH NESS

41. CLUE: BOO!

42. CAPRICORN

43. GOOD NIGHT!

44. CRYSTAL BALL

45. AQUARIUS

46. BLINK

47. MA GRIFFE

48. WHIZZARD

49. PISCES

50. DINNER TIME